FOZZIE'S
BIG BOOK OF
SIDESPLITTING JOKES
{PLEASE LAUGH}

STARRING JIM HENSON'S MUPPETS
Illustrated by Tim Kirk

Muppet Press/Random House

Copyright © 1981 by Henson Associates, Inc. The MUPPET SHOW, MUPPET, and MUPPET character names are trademarks of Henson Associates, Inc. All rights reserved under International and Pan-American Copyright Conventions. Published in the United States by Random House, Inc., New York, and simultaneously in Canada by Random House of Canada Limited, Toronto. A Muppet Press Book produced by Henson Organization Publishing in association with Random House, Inc.

Library of Congress Cataloging in Publication Data: Main entry under title: Fozzie's big book of sidesplitting jokes (please laugh) SUMMARY: Fozzie the bear delivers a monologue of jokes. 1. American wit and humor. 2. Wit and humor, Juvenile. [1. Jokes 2. Wit and humor] I. Kirk, Tim. PN6163.F68 818'.5407 80-23776 ISBN: 0-394-84675-3 Manufactured in the United States of America 2 3 4 5 6 7 8 9 0

Wocka, wocka! Too bad it's almost the end of my act. The bear is hot!

Listen, there was this lamb who needed a haircut . . .
So it went to the baa-baa shop!
Get it? Isn't that funneee?

Well, how about the guy who screwed a light bulb into a suit of armor?
He got a knight light!

Well, what about this? The other day a man asked me, "Would you rather an elephant or a gorilla attacked you?"

So I said, "I'd rather the elephant attacked the gorilla."
Aaaaaaaaaaah, I love that one!

Did you hear the one about
the happy guy who saw double?
    He was beside himself.
    Funneee!

    But seriously, a man walks
into a jeweler's shop and
says, "You know that
shockproof, waterproof,
dustproof deep-sea diver's
watch you sold me?
    "Well, it caught fire."
    Aaaaaaaahaaaa! I'm so
funneee!

ZZZzzz . . .

Hey, hey, you know I used to be a tap-dancer,
but I had to give it up.
I kept falling in the sink!

A man in a restaurant calls out, "Waiter, waiter!
What's this fly doing in my soup?"
The waiter answers, "Looks like the breaststroke, sir."
Aaaaaaaaah! I bet you never heard that one before!

Then the waiter says to the man, "How did you
find your steak, sir?"
The man says, "I lifted up the mushroom,
and there it was!"

Zz . . .

Oh, I love my jokes!
Hey, Kermit, Kermit, you know what kind
of fur you get from a skunk?
As *fur* as possible.

Or get this: A secretary says to his boss,
"The Invisible Man is at the door."
The boss says, "Tell him I can't see him."
Funnnneeee! Oh, I'm rolling now!

Did you hear the one about the cat who
swallowed a ball of yarn?
She had mittens! Wocka, wocka!

Show me
a tough guy,
and I'll show you
a coward.

I'm a tough guy.

I'm a
coward.

Hey, you in there! Why did the chicken go halfway across the road?

She wanted to lay it on the line!

Did you hear about the man who went to his doctor? "Doctor," he said, "I feel like a wrinkled dollar bill."

So the doctor said, "Go shopping. The change will do you good!"

Stop, Fozzie! *You're* too good!

You know, a woman once asked me how long the next bus would be.

So I said, "About twenty-five feet."

Then she said, "Do the buses run on time?"

So I said, "No, they run on wheels!"

Wocka, wocka!

But seriously, the guy who invented spaghetti was really using his noodle.

Spaghetti . . . noodle . . . ?

Oh, I love my act!

I once knew a carpenter who bought a box of nails and then threw them all away.

He said the heads were on the wrong end!

Wocka, wocka!

What do you know?
I weigh half an hour.

Did you hear the one about
the skyscraper?
Well, it's a tall story.

How long is the song "Soap,
Soap, Soap, Soap, Soap"?
Anybody know?
About five bars!
Yes! Oh, yes! This is my
"A" material!

So how about the bird whose cage fell apart?
All he could say was, "Cheap! Cheap! Cheap!"
Aaaaaah, the bear never misses!

I bet you don't know what a twack is.
It's something a twain runs on!
Get it? It's so funneee!

Why did the traffic light turn red?
So would you if you had to change in the middle of
the street!
Ha, ha, ha!

The other day a man said to me, "Hey, bear. Call
me a taxi."
So I said, "Certainly, sir. You are a taxi."
And *I* am so funneee!

How about the thief who stole two and a half miles
of elastic?
He was put away for a good, long stretch!
Oh, I am *so* funneee!

But seriously, it's ridiculous to hold a party
for chickens these days.

It's so hard to make hens meet. To make
hens meet! That slays me!

You know, pelicans eat anything that fits the bill!

Say, did you hear about the man who went to the
doctor and said, "Doctor, I feel like a dog."

So the doctor said, "Sit down and tell me about it."

"I can't," said the man. "I'm not allowed on the
furniture."

I love these jokes!

You know how to keep a skunk from smelling? Hold its nose!

Here's another boffo riddle: What did the water say to the bathtub? "I'll give you a ring on Saturday night!" Oh, that's good!

CITY PARK

NO
LITTERING
FISHING
SWIMMING
DOGS
COMICS

Why do squirrels spend so much time in trees?

To get away from all the nuts on the ground!

Then there's the one about the man who went to the doctor because his elbow hurt.

The doctor asks, "Have you ever had that pain before?"

The man says, "Yes."

So the doctor says, "Well, you've got it again!"

Aaaaaah, ha, ha!

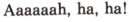

Moving right along . . . What did
the skunk say when the wind
changed direction?
"Ah, it's all coming back to
me now!"
Wocka, wocka!

A doctor examined a lady's hand. "I'm afraid it
will never be right," he said.
The lady said, "Oh no! Why not?"
So the doctor said, "Because it's your left hand."
Oh, is there no stopping this bear?

OY!

A man took a sip of coffee. "Yucch!" he said. "This coffee tastes like mud."

"It should," said the waitress. "It was *ground* this morning."

Hey, hey, you know what? A terrible noise woke me up this morning . . .
The crack of dawn!

Why did the golfer wear two pairs of trousers?
In case he got a hole in one!

Which reminds me, my mother told me the best way
to make my pants last.
She said, "Make your jacket first."
Funneee, Mom!

But seriously, there was
a man at my door selling
beehives.
I told him to buzz off!
Wocka, wocka!

Now get this—if
cowskins make good shoes,
what do banana skins make?
Good slippers!
Oh, the bear is too funny
for words!

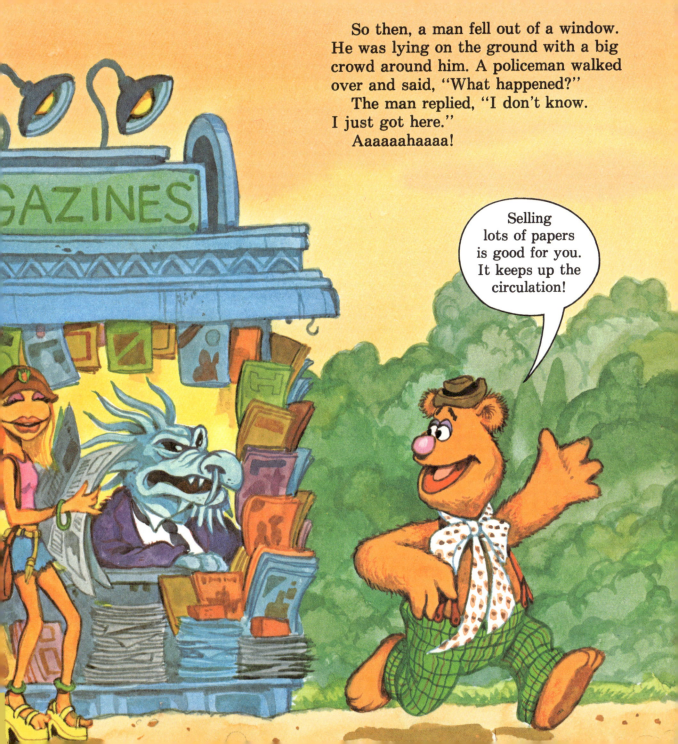

So then, a man fell out of a window. He was lying on the ground with a big crowd around him. A policeman walked over and said, "What happened?"

The man replied, "I don't know. I just got here."

Aaaaaahaaaa!

Selling lots of papers is good for you. It keeps up the circulation!

My last joke was good, but listen to this!
There was a mad scientist, see, and he crossed a chicken with a cement mixer. You know what he got?
A bricklayer!

I've lost my dog.

Gee, mister, that's too bad. Why don't you put an ad in the paper?

That wouldn't help. My dog can't read! Aaaaaaah!

Or what about the people who had a kitchen so small they could only use condensed milk?

Oh, Fozzie, where do you get them?

Hey, hey, listen to this one: Why is a dog dressed warmer in summer than in winter?

Because in winter he wears a fur coat, but in summer he wears a fur coat and pants!

Aaaaaaaahaaaaa!

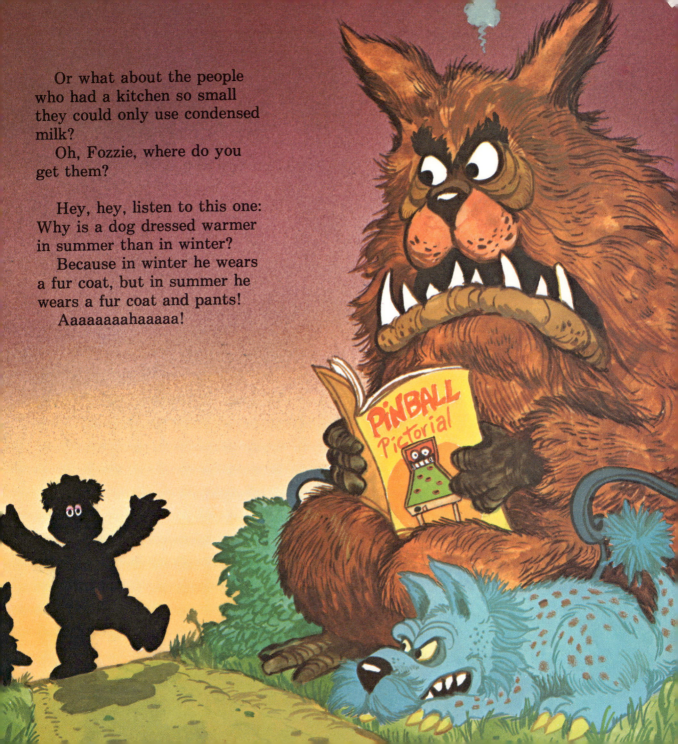

Hey, guess what? They're not going to grow bananas any longer.

They're long enough already!

Here's another hot one. What's black and white, black and white, and black and white and green? Give up?

Three skunks fighting over a pickle!

Waaaaaaah!

I *know* you loved that one, so get this: Did you hear about the scientist who crossed a monster with a computer?

She got a three-hundred-pound know-it-all!

Aaaaaaaaahaaaaa! Oh, the bear is great! The bear is hilarious!

The bear is out of jokes! So, that's all for now, folks!
I hope you loved me as much as I did! Thank you,
thank you! You were a wonderful audience! Wocka, wocka!